I can write a book series

I can write a book about Landforms

Bobbie Kalman

Crabtree Publishing Company
www.crabtreebooks.com

I can write a book series

Created by Bobbie Kalman

For Jennifer King, with thanks,
for enlightening me about the newest trends in education

Author and Editor-in-Chief
Bobbie Kalman

Editors
Kathy Middleton
Crystal Sikkens

Photo research
Bobbie Kalman

Educational consultant
Jennifer King

Prepress technician
Katherine Berti

Design
Bobbie Kalman
Katherine Berti
Samantha Crabtree
(logo and cover)

Print and production coordinator
Katherine Berti

Illustrations
Robert MacGregor: p. 27 (top left)

Photographs
Dreamstime: p. 9 (bottom right), 30 (bottom left inset)
Istockphoto: p. 11 (bottom left), 21 (bottom left inset)
Bobbie Kalman: back cover inset, p. 5 (top), 18 (bottom left inset), 29 (bottom)
Shutterstock: cover, logo, title page, p. 3, 4, 5 (bottom), 8, 9 (all except bottom right), 10, 11 (all except bottom left), 12–17, 18 (top and bottom book), 20, 21 (all except bottom left inset), 22–26, 27 (top right), 28, 29 (top and center), 30 (all except bottom left inset); photobank.ch: p. 19 (top)
Wikimedia Commons: p. 27 bottom (Claude Monet, *The Cliffs at Etretat*)

Library and Archives Canada Cataloguing in Publication

Kalman, Bobbie
I can write a book about landforms / Bobbie Kalman.

(I can write a book series)
Includes index.
Issued also in electronic format.
ISBN 978-0-7787-7992-6 (bound).--ISBN 978-0-7787-8001-4 (pbk.)

1. Landforms--Juvenile literature. 2. Geography--Authorship--Juvenile literature. 3. Composition (Language arts)--Juvenile literature. 4. English language--Composition and exercises--Juvenile literature. 5. Book design--Juvenile literature. I. Title. II. Series: Kalman, Bobbie. I can write a book.

GB402.K332 2012 j551.41 C2012-901149-5

Library of Congress Cataloging-in-Publication Data

Kalman, Bobbie.
I can write a book about landforms / Bobbie Kalman.
p. cm. -- (I can write a book series)
Includes index.

ISBN 978-0-7787-7992-6 (reinforced library binding : alk. paper) -- ISBN 978-0-7787-8001-4 (pbk. : alk. paper) -- ISBN 978-1-4271-7883-1 (electronic pdf) -- ISBN 978-1-4271-7998-2 (electronic html)
1. Landforms--Juvenile literature. 2. Creative writing--Juvenile literature. I. Title.

GB406.K256 2012
808.06'6551--dc23

2012005749

Crabtree Publishing Company

Printed in the USA/082018/HF20180705

www.crabtreebooks.com 1-800-387-7650

Published in Canada
Crabtree Publishing
616 Welland Ave.
St. Catharines, Ontario
L2M 5V6

Published in the United States
Crabtree Publishing
PMB 59051
350 Fifth Avenue, 59th Floor
New York, New York 10118

Published in the United Kingdom
Crabtree Publishing
Maritime House
Basin Road North, Hove
BN41 1WR

Published in Australia
Crabtree Publishing
3 Charles Street
Coburg North
VIC 3058

Table of contents

Will you write a book?

We read books for fun. We read books to learn about our world. Not all books are the same. **Fiction** books are stories created from someone's imagination. **Non-fiction** books are true. They can contain stories about real people or facts about animals, habitats, countries, machines, or sports. This non-fiction book shows you how to write and **publish** a non-fiction book about **landforms**. To publish is to share the final copy of your work with others. Landforms are **land formations**, or different shapes of land on Earth, such as mountains and caves.

You can explore landforms and teach others about them in your book. Which landform will you write about?

Bobbie's blog

Several years ago, I wrote a book called *Nicola's Floating Home*. Nicola had lived on a sailboat since she was a baby. To write this book, I spent a month with Nicola's family on an **island** in the Bahamas. An island is a landform with water all around it. It is my favorite landform, especially islands in the Bahamas, where I once lived and taught school before I became an **author**. Since then, I have written hundreds of non-fiction children's books, but I still think of myself as a teacher. I love writing books because I learn new things every day, and I can share what I have learned with students like you. By writing books, you can also be an author and a teacher. No matter what you do in life, you will do it better if you are a good writer.

Nicola and I had fun sailing from island to island in her sailboat home.

You can write your own book or write one together with some classmates.

Learning and teaching

When you write a book, you learn a lot about a subject. The more you learn, the more you will want to know. The more you know, the more you will want to discover. When you discover new things about the world, you will want to share what you have learned with others. Writing a book is a great way to share your knowledge! When others read your book, they will be learning from you. Besides being an author, you will be a teacher, too.

Parts of a book

Your teacher probably asks you to write reports for school. Writing a non-fiction book is like writing a report, but there are more parts and pages to a book. A book's pages are held together by a **cover**. A cover is the outside of the book. It is the first thing that people see. When people see a good cover, they will want to read the book. The cover shown here is the cover of this book. Your cover will be different (see page 30). What will you put on the cover of your book about landforms?

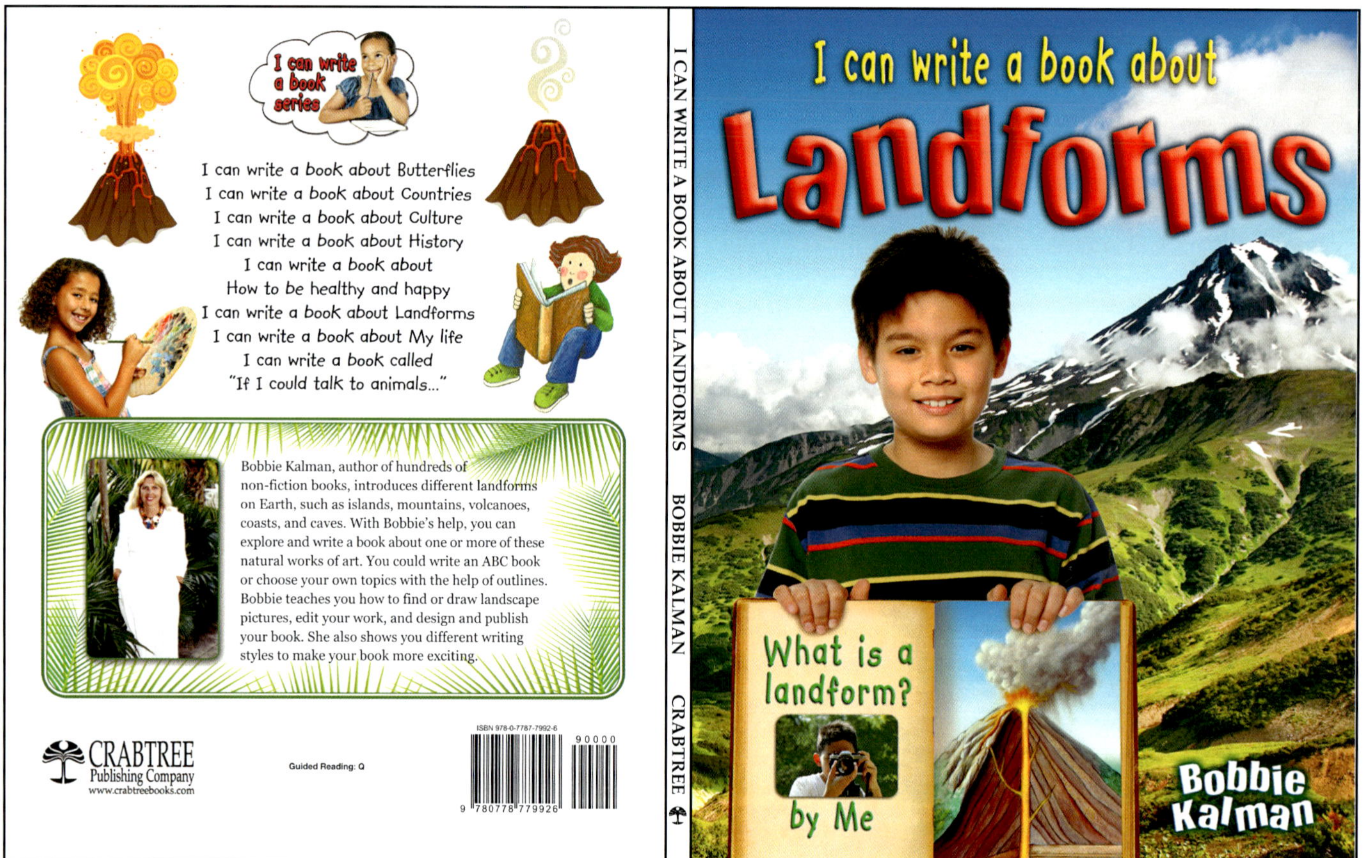

The back cover of the book may give you information about the author, ***publisher****, price, and other books written by the author.*

The ***spine*** *of the book has the title, author, and publisher's name. It helps you find a book on a bookshelf.*

The front cover of the book contains the title of the book and the name of the author. It catches your attention with an interesting title or a great picture or pictures.

The title page

The first page inside the cover is the **title page**. The picture on the right shows the title page of this book. What information does it give you?

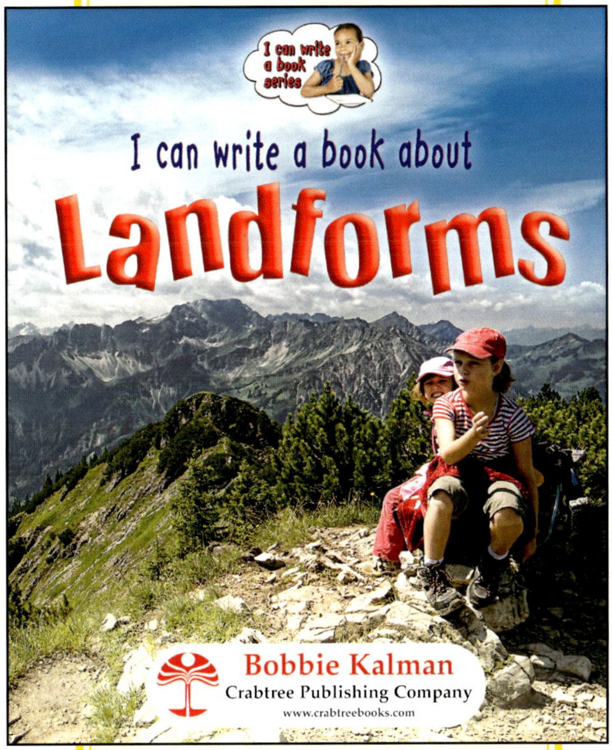

Copyright page

The second page in this book is the **copyright** page. Copyright means that people cannot copy all or parts of the book without the author's or publisher's permission. What else does it tell you? Turn to the copyright page in this book and find the following information:

- the names of the people who helped create this book
- the addresses of the publisher
- a **dedication**, or the words used to honor someone by placing his or her name in the book
- the **cataloging information**, a section of the page that tells the book's title, the name of the author, the year the book was published, and the type of book it is

The top page shows the title page, and the bottom one shows the table of contents of this book.

Contents, glossary, index

The **table of contents** gives the names of the **chapters**, or sections, in the book and the page numbers on which they begin. The **glossary** is a small dictionary that explains special words used in the book. The **index** is an alphabetical list of the topics in the book with page numbers telling where those topics are covered.

Table of contents

Landform words to know

The next four pages introduce you to the most important words about landforms. They give you information about landforms that will help you write your book. Important words are usually contained in a glossary at the end of a book. For your own book, you can do a picture dictionary with definitions underneath, like the examples on these pages, or a glossary without pictures, or both. (See pages 29 and 32 for how to write your glossary.)

*A **bay** is an area of ocean with land curving around it. A **beach** is a stretch of sand or stones that meets a body of water.*

*A **butte** is a narrow hill with a flat top and steep sides. A **mesa** is a wide mountain or hill with a flat top and steep sides.*

*A **canyon** is a deep, narrow, rocky area with steep sides, often with a river at the bottom.*

*A **cave** is an empty area under the ground or inside a cliff. A **cavern** is a large open area inside a cave. A **sea cave** is a large hole in the side of a cliff beside an ocean. A **stalactite** is a stone column that hangs from the ceiling of a cave. A **stalagmite** is a stone column that rises from the floor of a cave. Stalactites and stalagmites form from minerals in dripping water, which have built up into hard rock.*

*A **cliff** is a steep wall of rock at the edge of an ocean. A **sea stack** is a tall, steep rock that becomes separated from a cliff when a natural arch falls (see page 11).*

*A **continent** is one of Earth's seven huge areas of land (see page 12).*

*The **equator** is an imaginary line around the center of Earth that divides Earth into two equal parts.*

*A **fiord** or **fjord** is a long, narrow **inlet** between coasts with tall mountains. An inlet is a narrow body of water that flows from an ocean or lake.*

*A **coast** is the part of land beside an ocean. A **coastline** is the outline of a coast.*

*A **desert** is a dry area with very little rain. A **dune** is a hill of sand shaped by the wind.*

*A **glacier** is a slow-moving body of ice on mountains. This glacier is in the Himalayas, the highest mountains on Earth.*

More landform words

*A **hill** is a high area of land with sloping sides. A **karst** hill is made of **limestone**, a hard rock. These karst hills are called Chocolate Hills. They are in the Philippines in Asia.*

*An **island** is land with water all around it. Some islands are small, and some are big. This island is in a **tropical**, or hot, area. It is near the equator.*

*Landforms are different shapes of land on Earth. A **landscape** is all the features of land that a person sees, such as mountains and valleys. It can also be a picture that shows how the land looks. What features would you include if you were painting a landscape near your home?*

*A **mountain** is a high area of land with steep sides. A **peak** is the pointed top of a mountain. A **valley** is a low area between mountains or hills. Many valleys were formed by glaciers.*

A **natural arch** is a curved opening through a cliff or cave. It is also called a **natural bridge**. When the arch falls, the separated rock becomes a sea stack.

A **peninsula** is a piece of land that sticks out of a coast and has water around it on three sides.

A **rock formation** is a rock with an unusual shape. What animal does this rock resemble?

A **tsunami** is a series of long, high waves created by an earthquake or active volcano under water.

A **volcano** is an opening in the Earth's crust from which **lava** shoots out. It is also a mountain made from dried lava.

Most of Yellowstone National Park is inside the Yellowstone **Caldera**. A caldera is the large center of a huge volcano that collapsed. The Yellowstone Caldera contains mountains, canyons, valleys, and **hot springs**.

Big ideas about landforms

Non-fiction books contain **big ideas**, or important topics, about a subject. When you write a book about landforms, there are several topics you can explore. Here are some big ideas about landforms that will help you write your book. You can choose one topic or do them all. Are there landforms that you are studying at school? Those would be ideal to include in your book. You can write information about a subject the way you would in a report, or you can be more creative. You can add art, photography, stories, visits to landforms (see page 17), and activities to create a fun book, such as the alphabet book on pages 20–21.

Earth's biggest landforms

Continents are Earth's biggest landforms. The children below are painting the seven continents on Earth. Write the names of the continents in your notebook. Page 31 shows an ABC book about continents. Look for it in your library.

You and some friends could work on a book about continents and paint a huge mural to hang on your school wall. You could then take a photograph of the mural to include in your book.

Different landforms

Earth has many landforms. Some have been introduced on pages 8–11. Look at the pictures and definitions and decide which ones you want to write about in your book. You could also do a book about the forces that shape landforms, such as wind, water, volcanoes, earthquakes, animals, and people.

*This **Inukshuk** is on a mountain.*

Landforms near water

Coasts are land areas at the edges of oceans. Coasts have different shapes. You could write about the many features of coasts, such as sea caves, bays, cliffs, and beaches. You could also learn more about islands and write about the different ways they were formed.

Mountains on Earth

A book about mountains could include these topics:

- how mountains form and change
- different kinds of mountains
- different rocks in mountains
- Earth's biggest mountains
- mountains that are volcanoes
- big rock formations such as mesas

Volcanoes

Topics to explore about volcanoes are:

- different kinds of volcanoes
- looking inside Earth
- why and how volcanoes erupt
- how volcanoes shape the land

Getting started

Before you start writing, you need to plan what you want to write about. Picking landform topics that interest you will make writing your book more fun. Read the questions below and write your answers and thoughts in a "writer's notebook" that you will use to record the information you have learned.

Will I write my book on a computer or by hand?

Questions to ask myself

- What do I want to write about?
- How will I present the information?
- What do I know about landforms that I could share with others?
- What interests me the most about certain landforms? Which ones would I like to explore?
- Which landform has brought me the most fun? (e.g. skiing on a mountain, swimming at an island beach, hiking on a hill, looking at a volcano)
- How will I make my book exciting for others to read?
- How will I collect all the information I need?

Prewriting

- Choose landforms that are interesting to you and learn everything about them.
- Make an outline of the topics you will be writing about. Your outline will become your table of contents.
- Write some chapter headings you want to use and list ideas under each.

Remember!

- Make a list of landforms you want to write about.
- Write ways to make your book fun, such as using art, activities, and photos.
- Think about which landforms you would like to explore if you could.
- Compare landforms, such as hills, volcanoes, and mountains. How are they similar and different?

Sample outline one

What is a landform?
The biggest landforms
What are coasts?
Hills and mountains
The valleys below
Desert landforms
Deep canyons
Caves and caverns
What is a volcano?
Landforms quiz
Landform art

Sample outline two

What shapes the land?
Volcanoes create land
What is erosion?
Rivers carve through rocks
How do coasts change?
Wind and water change land
What are glaciers?
How do plants preserve land?
The rock cycle
How people shape the land

Will you work with some classmates and share ideas and information? You could write an ABC book and divide the letters so that everyone has different topics to cover, or you could choose the sample outlines shown here and do two or more books together. You can make your own outlines, too.

Researching information

There is information about landforms in this book, but you will need to **research**, or discover, more facts. Reading the books about different landforms, shown on page 31, is a good place to start. The books may be in your school or public library. You can also find information in other books, encyclopedias, and on the Internet. There are great videos to watch on landforms, as well! Use at least two sources for your research. Take notes, but be sure not to copy information word for word. Understand the information and then write it in your own words.

Ask your teacher if you can watch landform videos on the Internet. You could watch a volcano erupt or a tsunami hit a coast.

Your school library may have all the books you need. If not, you can visit the public library in your community. It will have many more books.

Explore the areas in your community with your parents or a group of friends and make a list of all the landforms you see.

*Include photographs of landforms you have visited and write about your experiences with them. Do some research on how this sea cave was shaped by **erosion**. Erosion is the wearing away of the surface of something by wind or water.*

Research review

- Use at least two research sources.
- Write research information in your own words.
- Interview someone in your family about their experiences with landforms.
- Include your own experiences and photographs while visiting landforms.

Take photographs of the landforms you see in your community.

Body of the book

Now that you have decided what kind of book you are writing and done some research, it is time to start writing the **body** of the book. The body of the book will contain the information you have learned and want to share with others.

Chapters, paragraphs, headings

You will find writing a book easier if you organize your ideas into small chapters called **spreads**. A spread is two pages that face each other. A **heading** tells you what a chapter is about. A chapter usually has several paragraphs. The paragraphs are separated by **subheadings**. A subheading is smaller than a chapter heading. It tells you what a paragraph is about. What is the heading of this chapter? What are the subheadings?

Bobbie's tip

In every book I write, I cover one main topic on each spread. When you write about a topic this way, your information, ideas, and pictures are much easier to organize. This book has fourteen spreads. How many topics and spreads will your book have?

Writing styles

To make your book more exciting to read, you could try writing some sections in the different writing styles shown on this page:

- **Informational** text gives information to readers. Most of this book is in informational text.
- **Narrative** text is written in story form. You could write a story about a trip to a landform, such as an island or mountain, and what you did there.
- **Instructional** text gives directions on how to do something. Examples of instructional text appear on the notebook pages in this book (see page 22).

Descriptive text uses the senses of sight, smell, hearing, taste, and touch to describe a place, thing, or event. Write a descriptive paragraph about the picnic these children are having in a mountain valley. What can they **see** around them? What can they **hear**? What do they **smell** and **taste**? What can they **touch**? What can they **feel** on their faces?

Landforms quiz

Take this quiz to see how much you have learned about landforms. Match the correct picture to each of these clues. The answers are on the next page.

Which landform...

1. shoots out hot melted rock?
2. has water at its edge and can be rocky or sandy?
3. was made from dead ocean animals called coral polyps?
4. is a large underground room?
5. is deeper than the land around it?
6. has sand or pebbles covered by shallow water?
7. has water on three sides?
8. is taller than a hill?
9. is mainly flat land?
10. is a rock with a weird shape?

A. hoodoo
B. beach
C. peninsula
D. coast
E. island
F. canyon
G. cavern
H. plain
I. mountain
J. volcano

Answers: 1-J; 2-D; 3-E; 4-G; 5-F; 6-B; 7-C; 8-I; 9-H; 10-A

28 29

The two pages shown here are from a book called Introducing Landforms, *shown on page 31. This spread contains a fun quiz. You can do one in your book, too, to test your readers about landforms.*

Writing an ABC book

Alphabet books are fun to write. They allow you to be extra creative. You can write about one landform on each spread or choose more than one. For example, a tsunami is a huge wave caused by an earthquake under water, so you could combine the letters T and U. The words on the chart below are suggestions to get you started. You can find a definition of most of the topics on pages 10–13.

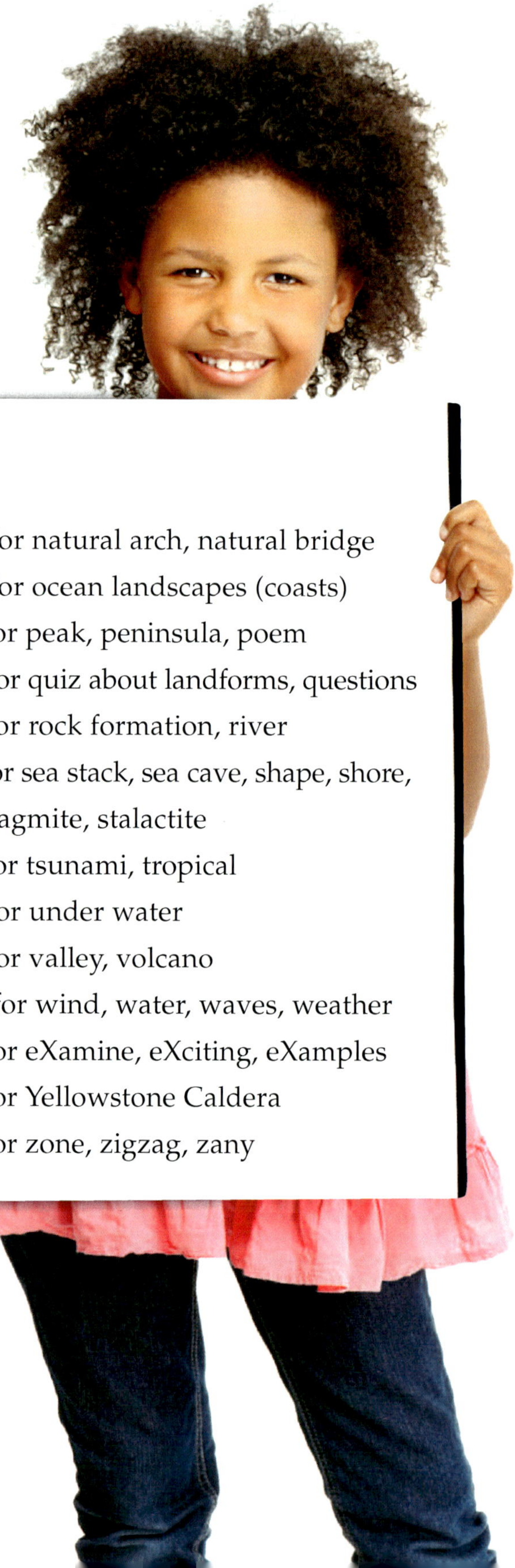

Landforms from A to Z

A is for "about" landforms, art
B is for bay, beach, butte
C is for continent, coast, cave (cavern), cliff, canyon
D is for desert, dune
E is for Earth, equator, erosion
F is for fiord, fire
G is for glacier, geyser, Greenland
H is for hill, Himalayas, hot springs
I is for island, ice, Iceland, Indonesia
J is for Japan
K is for Kilimanjaro, karst
L is for landscape, lava
M is for mountain, magma, mesa
N is for natural arch, natural bridge
O is for ocean landscapes (coasts)
P is for peak, peninsula, poem
Q is for quiz about landforms, questions
R is for rock formation, river
S is for sea stack, sea cave, shape, shore, stalagmite, stalactite
T is for tsunami, tropical
U is for under water
V is for valley, volcano
W is for wind, water, waves, weather
X is for eXamine, eXciting, eXamples
Y is for Yellowstone Caldera
Z is for zone, zigzag, zany

You may need to be extra creative with some letters. For the letter Q, for example, you could write a quiz and test your friends to see how much they know about landforms (see page 19). For P, you could write a poem about how a landform made you feel when you visited it. What will you write for the letters X and Z?

I is for island.

Questions and ideas about islands:

- How can people reach islands if there is water all around them?
- How are islands formed?
- Which is the biggest island on Earth? (It's name starts with G.)
- Write about Iceland or Indonesia (two island countries).
- Write a poem about animals you saw on an island you visited.
- Include photographs taken of you on an island or draw pictures.
- Write **captions** to explain what is happening in your pictures.

M is for mountain.

Most mountains have steep sides that rise almost straight up from the ground. Are there mountains near your home that you could climb or paint as a landscape?

Write about your experience climbing a mountain or imagine what it would be like to reach the top of the Himalayas, the highest mountains on Earth.

Fonts or handwriting?

There are different ways to write. If you are using a computer, you have many choices. If you are writing your book by hand, you can use colors and different ways of writing that look like the words on a computer.

What is a font?

A **font** is a style of type. Most of this book is written in a **plain text** font, but you will notice other kinds of fonts, as well. Words that are written in a **boldface**, or thick black, font are words that may be new to you. Sometimes they are explained on the page, and sometimes they are defined in the glossary of the book. The headings and subheadings are in larger type. A different font is used to make them stand out from the rest of the text. Headings may also be in color. Choose colors that match the pictures on the pages.

Captions and fact boxes

The text that gives you information about a picture is called a caption. The captions in this book are written in *italics*. Letters in italics slant to the right. Captions are smaller than plain text. **Fact boxes** bring attention to special information, ask questions, or give instructions. There are several fact boxes in this book. They are shown on notebook pages, like the one above.

Choosing fonts

- If you are writing your book on a computer, try using some different fonts.
- Choose a plain text font that is easy to read.
- Choose heading fonts that suit your subject.
- If you are writing your book by hand, use a thick pencil, pen, or marker to make **boldfaced** words.
- Write captions by *slanting* your words to look like an *italic* font.
- For headings, use markers or colored pencils.

Practice caption writing

Write captions for the pictures on this page. Use your imagination! What is the girl saying to these mountain sheep? What is the boy thinking as he looks out on the ocean? What kind of animal does the red rock formation below resemble?

Font review

Plain text font is used to write most of the information in the book.

Boldface font is used to introduce new words.

Italic font is used for writing captions. A caption tells what is happening in a picture.

This font is used in fact boxes that give you extra information or special directions.

Chapter headings are in large colored type.

Subheadings are smaller than chapter headings. They may also be in color.

Revising and editing

Once you have written your **draft**, or first try at writing your book, it is time to read it to yourself. While reading, ask yourself these questions:

- Did I say what I wanted to say?
- Have I included my own observations or experiences with landforms?
- Have I repeated some information that needs to be taken out?
- Do my captions give interesting information? Do they describe what is happening in the pictures?
- Do my sentences make sense?
- Did I use **comparisons** to make my work more interesting and accurate?
- Have I asked questions to make my readers think?
- How can I **revise**, or rewrite, my book to make it better?

Ask a parent or your teacher to help you organize and improve your work.

Share your draft

- After you have read your draft and made some changes, it is time to share it with others.
- Read your draft loudly and clearly at least twice. Ask your classmates what they liked or did not understand.
- Listen to their suggestions: What questions did they ask? What parts of your draft were not clear? What changes did they feel you could make?
- Other students can then read their drafts. Use the checklists on the opposite page to help improve your drafts.

Editing checklist

Editing is checking information to make sure it is clear and correct.

- Have you covered all the information you intended to?
- Are your chapters in the best order to explain your subject?
- Do your headings reflect the information in your paragraphs?
- Have you used new and interesting words?

Proofreading checklist

Proofreading is checking for errors such as spelling and typing mistakes, capital letters, and punctuation.

- Do your sentences make sense?
- Have you used the correct **punctuation** and capitals?
- Have you spelled names and other words correctly?

Why all the questions?

How do questions help you?

- They help you review what you have written and think about what you still need to write.
- They help you think of other ideas to include in your book.
- They tell you what you have not explained clearly.

Designing your book

Designing your book is planning how it will look. If your design is attractive, people will want to read your book. Writing text in a certain way, such as in fact boxes, is part of design. The other very important part is including **visuals**, or different kinds of pictures. Some visuals, such as diagrams, help your readers understand how something works. Other visuals make your book look good. Here are some ways to find or create visuals for your book.

Take photographs of landforms near your home or use photos you have taken on vacation.

Draw or paint a landscape, such as a beach where you spent your vacation.

Use your imagination and create a landscape picture like this one, which is made up of people's faces. Which landforms make up this picture? How many faces can you see? Did you look in the ocean, too?

Draw diagrams and label them

Draw and label diagrams that will help your readers understand your information. One diagram shows Earth's layers. The other shows how a volcano **erupts**, or becomes active.

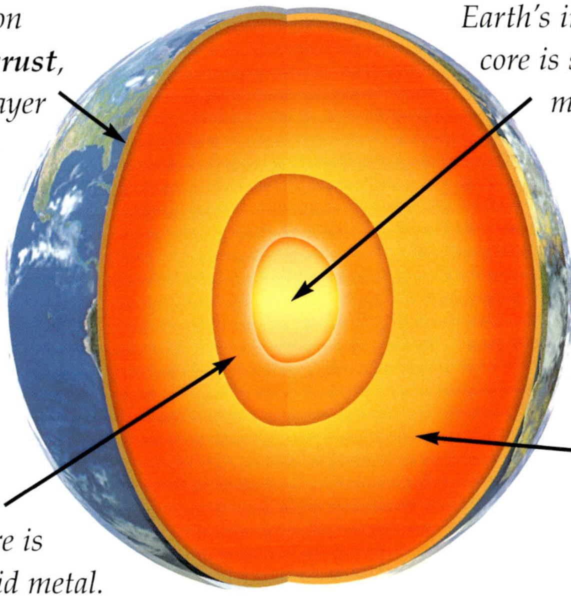

Download pictures

Ask a parent or teacher to show you how to download pictures from the Internet. Do a search of the kinds of photographs or art you need. Many photographs and works of art are in the **public domain**, which means they can be used by anyone. Make sure you include the **source**, or where you found the picture. Wikimedia Commons has many pictures you can download. Print or photocopy the pictures, cut them out, and place them in your book.

This landscape painting, called The Cliffs at Etretat, *shows a cliff, sea stack, and natural arch. The picture was painted by French artist Claude Monet in 1885. The copyright page in this book will tell you where to find this picture.*

Publishing your book

Publishing your book is the last step. Does your library have a publishing program for students? Many schools place the books students have written in the library for other students to read. If you did your book on the computer, you could make an eBook that many students could enjoy. Before you publish your book on the computer or by hand, you will need to complete all the parts of the book you learned about on pages 6 and 7: the copyright page; table of contents; the glossary; and index. The final step will be to design a cover and title page. Find all these pages in this book and use them to help you.

You may need to ask a parent or teacher to help you finish designing your book on a computer.

Copyright page

Your copyright page will include the names of the people who helped you with your book, the books you used for research, and the sources for pictures you downloaded. You can also include a dedication on this page. To whom will you dedicate your book?

Table of contents

Your table of contents is a list of the headings of the chapters in your book. Their page numbers are placed at the right or left of the headings. Your table of contents is a revised list of your outline. (See the table of contents of this book on page 3.)

Glossary

There is a picture dictionary on pages 10-13 in this book, but your glossary can just be words, like the glossary on page 32. Use a dictionary to help you define words you did not know or your readers may not know. Sort your glossary in alphabetical order.

Index

The index is a list of the names and subjects that readers look for in books. It is in alphabetical order and gives the page numbers of where the subjects are in the book. The index on page 32 will help you write the index for your book.

Bobbie's reminder

The pages shown above are very important because they help your reader find and understand information in your book. They also thank people who helped you edit, proofread, and design your book, as well as credit the sources of photographs and art. You can also include a **bibliography**, or a list of books and their authors, that you used for your research. Use the copyright page in this book to help you write your own.

Cover and title page

There are different ways to present your book to your readers. In some schools, the teacher or librarian has ways of **binding**, or tying, the pages of books together so other students can read the book without losing any of the pages. One of the easiest ways to keep your book together is to photocopy all your pages and then slip each one into a binder with plastic sleeves. You can put your cover pages into the plastic pockets on the outside of the binders. The spine will also have a thin plastic pocket for your title. Below is a sample front and back cover. On the right is a title page.

title page

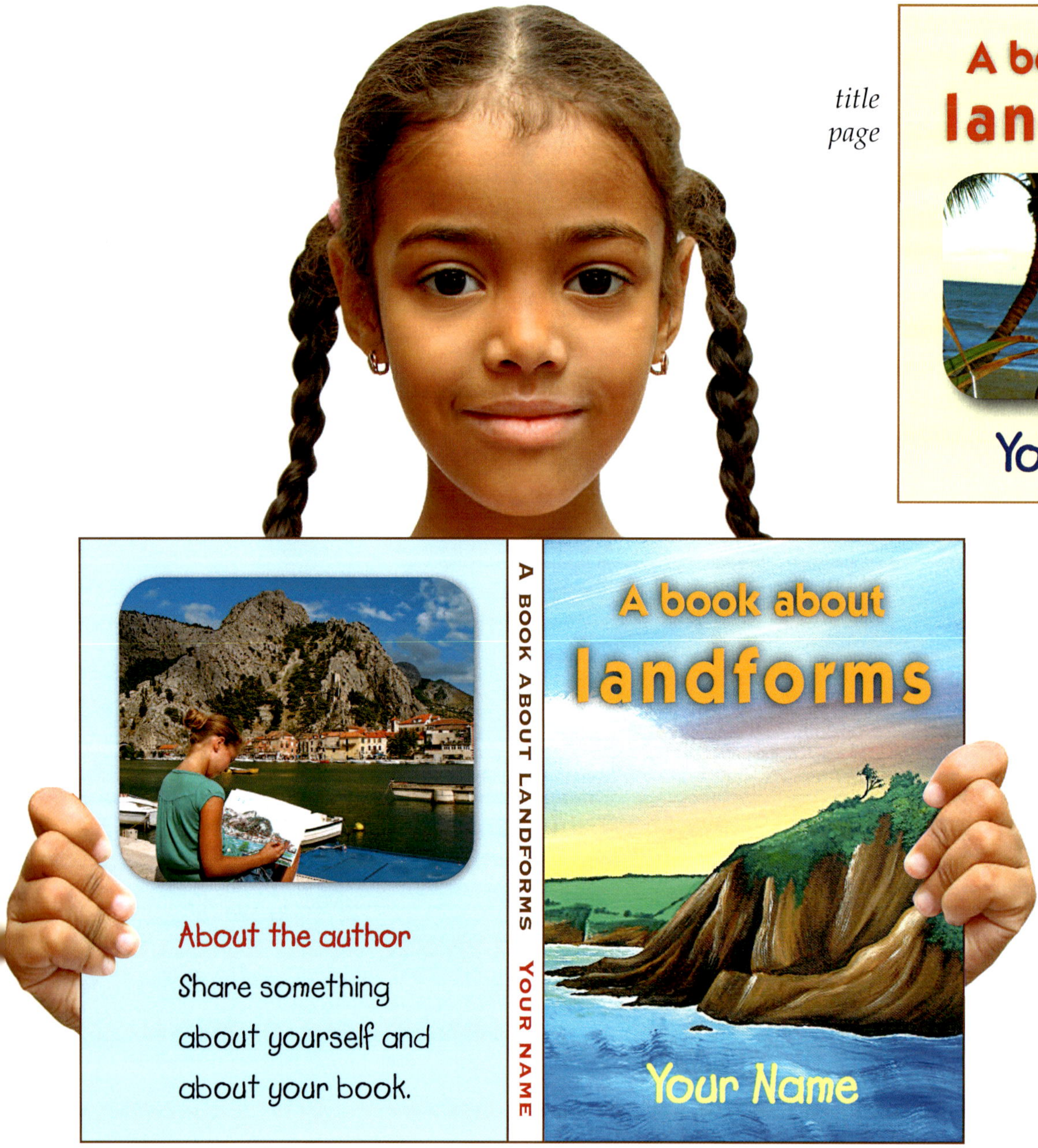

plastic binders

Books to read

The books shown here were written by me, Bobbie Kalman. They are about landforms. You can use the ABC book to help you write your own ABC book. You can find these books in your school or public library.

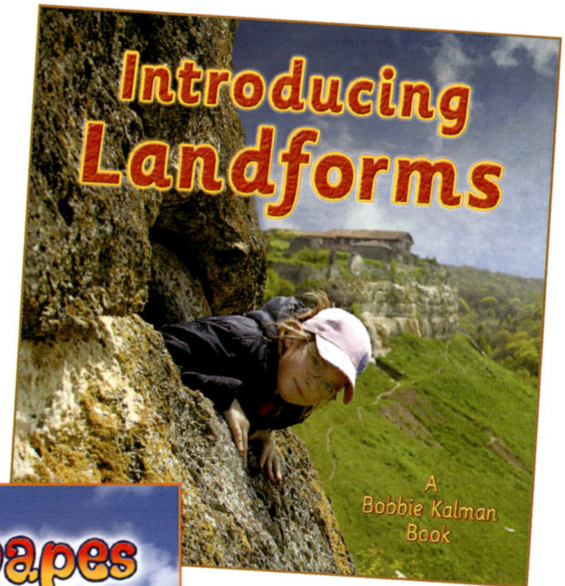

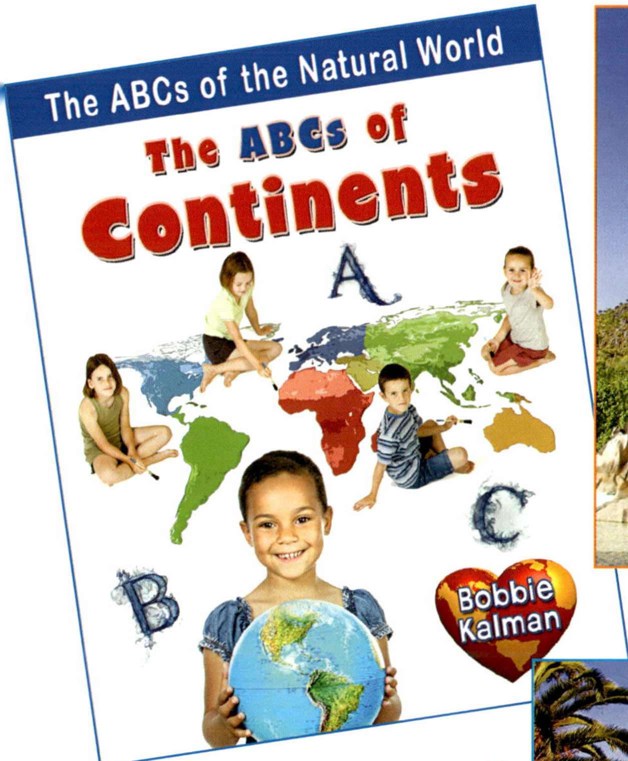

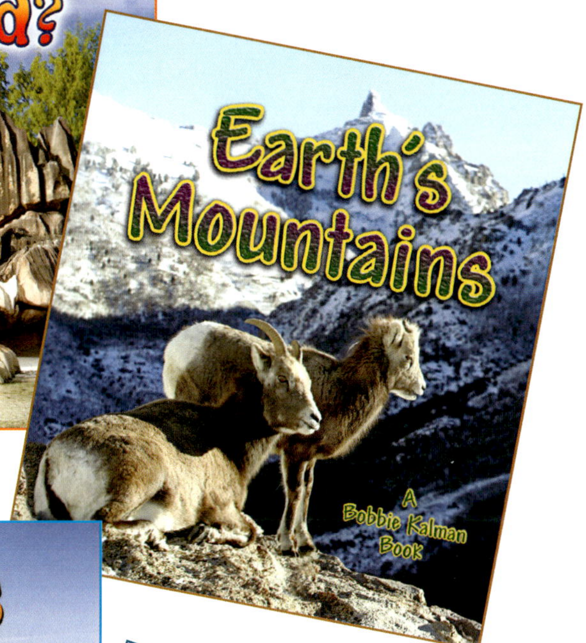

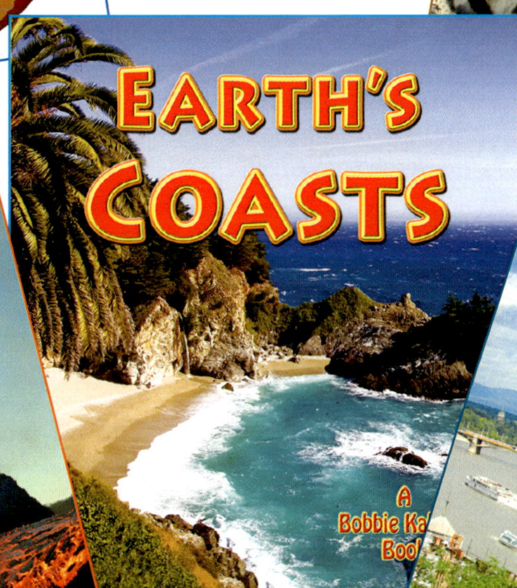

Glossary

Note: Some boldfaced words are defined where they appear in the book.

bibliography A list of the books and sources used for research

comparison The act of determining the likenesses and differences of a place, structure, or event

descriptive A writing style that uses the five senses of sight, hearing, smell, taste, and touch

editing Reading, checking facts, and revising parts of someone's writing

hot spring A source of water that flows up from the ground, which is heated naturally from inside the earth

informational A writing style that gives information about something

instructional A writing style that gives instructions or directions on how to do something

narrative A writing style that tells something in story form

proofreading Checking a book for correct spelling, grammar, and punctuation

publisher A person or company that is responsible for printing and distributing a written book, magazine, or newspaper

punctuation The use of marks, such as periods or commas, to make the meaning of a sentence clear

visuals Pictures such as maps, artwork, and photographs, used to illustrate information and design a book

Index